THE HISTORY OF THE PITTSBURGH STEELERS

THE HISTORY OF THE
PITTSBURGH

Published by Creative Education
123 South Broad Street
Mankato, Minnesota 56001
Creative Education is an imprint of The Creative Company.

DESIGN AND PRODUCTION BY **EVANSDAY DESIGN**

LIBRARY OF CONGRESS CATALOGING-IN-PUBLICATION DATA

Schmalzbauer, Adam.
The history of the Pittsburgh Steelers / by Adam Schmalzbauer.
p. cm. — (NFL today)
Summary: Traces the history of the team from
its beginnings through 2003.
ISBN 1-58341-310-3
1. Pittsburgh Steelers (Football team)—History—Juvenile literature.
[1. Pittsburgh Steelers (Football team)—History.
2. Football—History.] I. Title. II. Series.

GV956.P57S36 2004
796.332'64'0974886—dc22   2003065043

First edition

9 8 7 6 5 4 3 2 1

COVER PHOTO: linebacker Kendrell Bell

PHOTOGRAPHS BY
AP/Wide World Photos, Corbis (Bettmann, Reuters, UPI/Corbis-Bettmann), Getty Images,
Icon Sports Media Inc., SportsChrome USA

PITTSBURGH, PENNSYLVANIA, WAS FOUNDED ON THE SITE OF THE NATIVE AMERICAN TOWN SHANNOPIN, A LATE 17TH-CENTURY FUR-TRADING POST. ITS PRIME LOCATION AT THE JUNCTION OF THE ALLEGHENY, MONONGAHELA, AND OHIO RIVERS MADE IT AN IMPORTANT SHIPPING PORT, AND PITTSBURGH RAPIDLY GREW INTO A MAJOR INDUSTRIAL CENTER. BY THE 1800S, PITTSBURGH WAS KNOWN AS AMERICA'S "STEEL CITY" DUE TO ITS TREMENDOUS STEEL INDUSTRY. IN 1933, A WEALTHY SPORTS FAN NAMED ARTHUR ROONEY BROUGHT THE STEEL CITY A FRANCHISE IN THE NATIONAL FOOTBALL LEAGUE (NFL). THE TEAM WAS INITIALLY CALLED THE PIRATES—JUST LIKE ROONEY'S FAVORITE PROFESSIONAL BASEBALL TEAM, THE PITTSBURGH PIRATES—BUT THE OWNER SOON DECIDED TO CHANGE THE CLUB'S NAME TO THE STEELERS. THE HARDWORKING TEAM IN YELLOW AND BLACK HAS PLAYED A MAJOR ROLE IN PRO FOOTBALL HISTORY EVER SINCE.

[Linebacker Andy Russell]

ROONEY'S PIRATES WOULD eventually enjoy great success, but not early on. The club set sail in 1933 and finished last in the NFL's Eastern Division. The team's play wasn't the only thing that was ugly, however. Rooney had outfitted his players in ridiculous striped jerseys, leading opposing players to call them "jailbirds." Rooney soon decked his team out in new jerseys, but the team's poor performance on the field was not so readily solved.

The Pirates continued to struggle throughout the 1930s. Fans saw some valiant performances by such players as Hall of Fame running backs Byron "Whizzer" White and Johnny "Blood" McNally (who took his very first kick return for Pittsburgh 92 yards for a touchdown), but it wasn't enough. The team posted a losing record every season during the decade.

As a rookie, quick halfback Byron "Whizzer" White led the league in rushing during the 1938 season^

In 1940, Rooney hired Bert Bell as coach of the newly named Steelers. Unfortunately, neither the coach nor the name change seemed to help. Pittsburgh's 1–9–1 record in 1940 earned it last place yet again. As Rooney said, "We've got a new team, a new coach, a new nickname, and new uniforms, but they look like the same old Pirates to me."

Rooney then turned to coach Walt Kiesling, who orchestrated a remarkable turnaround in 1942, guiding the Steelers to their first winning season (7–4). Since many NFL players—including Steelers star running back Bill Dudley—had left football to serve their country in World War II, Pittsburgh merged with the Philadelphia Eagles for the 1943 season. In their one season together, the "Steagles" went 5–4–1. Then, despite featuring such all-time NFL greats as Dudley and defensive tackle Ernie Stautner, the Steelers enjoyed only two winning seasons between 1944 and 1956.

In 1957, Kiesling was fired and replaced by former Detroit Lions coach Ray Parker. After the Steelers went just 6–6 in 1957, Coach Parker made a trade to obtain his old quarterback from Detroit: Bobby Layne. Layne was a tough and confident leader. "I never lost a game," he once told a reporter. "I just ran out of time."

Quarterback Bobby Layne was a fearless leader with a knack for producing victory in close games^

To further boost his offense, Coach Parker then struck a trade with the San Francisco 49ers, bringing running back John Henry Johnson to Pittsburgh. The move turned out to be a smart one as the 230-pound Johnson rushed for more than 4,300 yards in six seasons in Pittsburgh—numbers that would eventually earn him a place in the Pro Football Hall of Fame.

With a talented roster that also included receiver Buddy Dial, the Steelers posted four winning records in their next eight seasons. They made their strongest run at an NFL championship in 1962, when they went 9–5 and made the playoffs. The Steelers lasted only one round in the playoffs, however, falling to Detroit 17–10. Layne and star defensive tackle Gene "Big Daddy" Lipscomb retired after that, and things quickly went downhill in Pittsburgh. It would be nearly a decade before the Steelers would enjoy another winning season.

Bruiser John Henry Johnson was the first Steelers player to run for 1,000 yards in a season

IN 1969, FORMER Baltimore Colts assistant Chuck Noll was named Pittsburgh's new head coach. A patient leader, Noll knew the best way to build a real "team of steel" in Pittsburgh would be through the NFL Draft. Noll made his first big move by drafting 6-foot-4 and 280-pound defensive tackle Joe Greene in 1969. Despite Greene's mammoth size, fans were initially skeptical of the draft choice. As one fan put it, "They had a shot at every college player in the country except three and managed to come up with a guy nobody ever heard of."

Fans around the NFL would hear of "Mean Joe" Greene soon enough. Greene quickly earned a reputation for his ferocious style of play, captivating fans with such performances as a 1972 game in which he sacked the quarterback five times. Elected to the Pro Bowl 10 times, Greene

Mighty tackle Joe Greene led the Steelers in sacks (11) in 1972, the first season the team recorded them.^

Franco Harris was a big-play rusher who scored 17 touchdowns in 19 career playoff games

Passer Terry Bradshaw led Pittsburgh to four NFL titles^

Lynn Swann was famous for his amazing leaping ability^

would team with another 1969 draft pick—defensive end L.C. Greenwood—to anchor a mighty defense that became known as the "Steel Curtain."

After the Steelers went just 1–13 in 1969, Noll continued to patiently add pieces to his championship puzzle. In 1970, he selected a strong-armed quarterback named Terry Bradshaw with the first overall pick in the NFL Draft. Then, in 1972, Noll struck gold in the draft again by selecting powerful young running back Franco Harris.

With Bradshaw, Harris, and linebacker Jack Ham added to the mix, the Steelers finally broke out of their slump in 1972. After suffering eight straight losing seasons, Pittsburgh roared to an 11–3 record to win the American Football Conference (AFC) Central Division and make the playoffs. Harris led the way by charging for more than 100 yards in six straight games, tying an NFL record. "Franco was the key man on our ball club," Greene later noted. "We were coming on every year in the 1970s, getting better and better. All we needed was the catalyst, and Franco was it."

IN 1973, THE STEELERS rolled to a 10–4 record. After Pittsburgh lost in the first round of the playoffs, Coach Noll concentrated his draft magic one more time. From fearsome linebacker Jack Lambert and dependable center "Iron" Mike Webster, to sure-handed receivers Lynn Swann and John Stallworth, Noll drafted a crew in 1974 that would combine for 24 Pro Bowl appearances and 16 Super Bowl rings.

Arthur Rooney had waited more than 40 years for his team to capture the ultimate football prize, but the wait was finally over. Propelled by their draft success, the 1974 Steelers culminated 41 years of Pittsburgh pride with a 16–6 Super Bowl victory over the Minnesota Vikings. "Today's win made all the other years worth it," said Rooney, his voice quivering with emotion. "I am happy for the coaches and players, but I'm especially happy for the Pittsburgh fans. They deserved this."

Known for his great instincts, linebacker Jack Ham (left) always seemed to be around the ball. ^

In 14 seasons wearing gold and black, John Stallworth caught a club-record 63 touchdown passes

Pittsburgh fans remained happy in 1975 as the Steelers won 11 straight games and then beat the Dallas Cowboys 21–17 to repeat as Super Bowl champs. The Steelers almost "three-peated" in 1976, winning 10 games in a row before losing to the Oakland Raiders in the AFC championship game. A year later, the Steelers seemed to run out of steam, finishing 9–5 and making a quick playoff exit.

But just when Pittsburgh's opponents were ready to breathe a sigh of relief, the Steelers cemented their legacy as the "Team of the '70s" by winning two more Super Bowls. In 1978, they went 14–2 and topped the Cowboys 35–31 for the championship. A year later, the Steelers crushed the Los Angeles Rams 31–19. Bradshaw—who was named the Most Valuable Player (MVP) of both of those Super Bowls—became the first (and still only) quarterback to earn four Super Bowl rings.

"I should say it has to be our best team," Bradshaw said of the 1979 team. "We had all this pressure on us. Everyone has been shooting at us for the past eight years. That's a tremendous strain. This is our fourth Super Bowl win, something nobody else has ever done before. We were on the verge of really setting history—and we accomplished it."

Iron-man center Mike Webster anchored the Steelers' offensive line for 15 terrific seasons

AS THE STEELERS entered the 1980s, the accomplished members of the "Team of the '70s" retired one by one. After a couple of mediocre seasons, Pittsburgh rose up once more to reach the 1984 AFC championship game. The team had talent—including rookie receiver Louis Lipps and safety Donnie Shell—but as quarterback Dan Marino and the Miami Dolphins picked the Steelers apart 45–28, it was obvious that Pittsburgh needed a talented quarterback.

Early '80s standout Louis Lipps reminded Pittsburgh fans of Lynn Swann with his acrobatic grabs ^

In the best season of his Steelers career (1990), quarterback Bubby Brister tossed 20 touchdown passes.

Coach Noll believed he had found that quarterback by drafting Walter "Bubby" Brister in 1986. Brister led his teammates mostly through action. "You can talk all you want, but if you don't get the job done, then talk doesn't mean a thing," he said. "You set certain standards by your performance, and if you are respected by your teammates, they will try to meet those standards.... Talking a good game doesn't cut it. Being a producer is what it's all about."

Brister was the team's starting quarterback by 1988 and quickly established himself as Pittsburgh's top "producer." Before the 1989 season, he scribbled "PLAYOFFS 89" on a locker room chalkboard. Then he went out and made that a reality, leading the Steelers to a 9–7 record and a return to the postseason.

The Steelers fell behind the Houston Oilers in the first round of the playoffs, but Brister rallied his troops for a late scoring drive that sent the contest to overtime. A few minutes later, Steelers kicker Gary Anderson booted a 50-yard field goal to give Pittsburgh a 26–23 victory. A loss to the Denver Broncos the following week ended the team's season, but fans were certain that better times lay ahead.

THE STEELERS STARTED slowly in the 1990s. After the team missed the playoffs in 1990 and 1991, Coach Noll decided to call it quits. The coaching reins were then handed to former NFL linebacker and Pittsburgh native Bill Cowher, who had grown up near the Steelers' home, Three Rivers Stadium. "I still remember registering him for Pop Warner football," said Cowher's father Laird. "Now that same boy is back home coaching the hometown team I've lived and died for my whole life. What a fairy tale."

Coach Cowher improved on that fairy tale in 1992 by leading the Steelers to an 11–5 record and winning NFL Coach of the Year honors. Then, behind such hard-hitting defensive stars as linebacker Greg Lloyd and cornerback Rod Woodson, the Steelers found themselves knocking on the door to the Super Bowl in 1993 and 1994, making the playoffs each year.

One of the 1990s' most dominant defensive players, Rod Woodson was also a star kick returner

"The Bus," Jerome Bettis, rumbled for 1,000 or more yards every season from 1996 to 2001^

In 1995, the Steelers featured a new offensive weapon: rookie Kordell Stewart. The young athlete from the University of Colorado displayed such amazing versatility that the team program listed his position as "quarterback/running back/wide receiver." Nicknamed "Slash" because of all the slashes in his position listing, Stewart might throw a pass to receiver Yancey Thigpen on one play, then line up at wide receiver himself and catch a pass from quarterback Neil O'Donnell on the next play. With Stewart on board, Pittsburgh went 13–3 in 1995 and charged to the Super Bowl.

Although the Steelers lost to the Cowboys in the Super Bowl, they remained an AFC heavyweight in the seasons that followed. Even though Woodson and several other standouts soon left town, new talent continued to emerge. In 1996, Jerome Bettis—a 5-foot-11 and 250-pound running back nicknamed "the Bus"—charged for 1,431 yards. With Bettis, Stewart, and Thigpen leading the offense, the Steelers made the playoffs in 1996 and 1997.

By 2001, Stewart was throwing the ball to the deadly receiving duo of Plaxico Burress and Hines Ward. The 6-foot-5 Burress was known for his graceful style and leaping ability, while the short but tough Ward was perhaps best known for his devastating blocks. Both players posted more than 1,000 receiving yards as Pittsburgh went 13–3. "We're the best tandem in football," Burress said boldly.

Although the Steelers came up short of the Super Bowl that season and the two that followed, the Pittsburgh faithful continued to find reasons for optimism. With Coach Cowher guiding a wealth of offensive talent—including newly acquired running back Duce Staley—and such ferocious defenders as linebackers Joey Porter and Kendrell Bell, the Steelers appeared ready to continue their rule of the AFC North Division for many seasons to come.

The Pittsburgh Steelers' history is a long and rich one that includes four Super Bowl victories and a list of legendary names such as McNally, Greene, Bradshaw, and Lambert. As today's gridiron heroes in yellow and black carry on the football tradition begun by Art Rooney more than seven decades ago, fans in the Steel City continue to believe that the team's fifth world championship is just around the corner.

With his huge wingspan and great speed, Plaxico Burress was a dangerous offensive threat.

INDEX >